C000185889

Tab's kitten

Story written by Gill Munton
Illustrated by Tim Archbold

Speed Sounds

Consonants   *Ask children to say the sounds.*

f	l	m	n	r	s	v	z	**sh**	**th**	**ng**
ff	ll		**nn**	rr	ss	ve	zz			**nk**
	le		kn				s			

b	c	d	g	h	j	p	**qu**	t	w	x	y	ch
bb	k	dd	gg			pp		**tt**	wh			**tch**
	ck											

Each box contains one sound but sometimes more than one grapheme.
Focus graphemes for this story are **circled**.

4

Vowels *Ask children to say the sounds in and out of order.*

a	e ea	i	o	u	ay	ee y	igh	ow
at	hen	in	on	up	day	see	high	blow

oo	oo	ar	or	air	ir	ou	oy
zoo	look	car	for	fair	whirl	shout	boy

Story Green Words

Ask children to read the words first in Fred Talk and then say the word.

Tab   Meg   Finn   sniff   tum   stretch   bath

nap

Ask children to say the syllables and then read the whole word.

kitt|en

Ask children to read the root first and then the whole word with the suffix.

stand → stands   trot → trots

Red Words

Ask children to practise reading the words across the rows, down the columns and in and out of order clearly and quickly.

he	she	to	no
call	her	I've	the
we	me	all	my
want	you	your	I've

Tab's kitten

Tab the cat has had a kitten.
"Tab! Tab!

I've got fish and milk!"
calls Meg.

Tab trots to Meg.
The kitten trots along as well.

sniff
sniff

Tab has the fish.

The kitten drinks the milk.

Tab's tum is full.
She has a quick nap.

The kitten runs off.

Tab stands up to stretch her long legs.

No kitten!

Is he in the box?

No!

Is he in the bath?

No!

Is he on Meg's bed?

No ...

Yes, he is!

He is with Finn!

Questions to talk about

Ask children to TTYP for each question using 'Fastest finger' (FF) or 'Have a think' (HaT).

p.8 (HaT) Do you remember where Meg bought Tab the cat?

p.11 (FF) What does the kitten do while Tab has a nap?

p.12 (FF) Where does Tab search for the kitten?

p.13 (HaT) How do you think Tab feels when she finds the kitten?